ALSO BY OKSANA ZABUZHKO
(AVAILABLE IN ENGLISH)

Your Ad Could Go Here

Museum of Abandoned Secrets

Fieldwork in Ukrainian Sex

A Kingdom of Statues

From Three Worlds (co-editor)

Girls

SELECTED POEMS

ARROWSMITH
PRESS

Selected Poems
Oksana Zabuzhko
© 2020 Arrowsmith Press
All Rights Reserved

ISBN: 978-1-7346416-3-9

Boston — New York — San Francisco — Baghdad
San Juan — Kyiv — Istanbul — Santiago, Chile
Beijing — Paris — London — Cairo — Madrid
Milan — Melbourne — Jerusalem — Darfur

11 Chestnut St.
Medford, MA 02155

arrowsmithpress@gmail.com
www.arrowsmithpress.com

The thirty-second Arrowsmith book was typeset & designed
by Ezra Fox for Askold Melnyczuk & Alex Johnson
in Baskerville & Plantagenet Cherokee typeface

Cover image by Rostyslav Luzhetskyy

Most of the poems here appeared in *A Kingdom of Fallen Statues*,
edited by Marko Carynnyk (Wellspring, Toronto, 1996).
Individual poems originally appeared in *Agni, Harvard Review,
Massachusetts Review, Ploughshares, Poetry Miscellany* & in the anthology
From Three Worlds (New Ukrainian Writing) edited by Ed Hogan,
Askold Melnyczuk, Michael M. Naydan, Mykola Riabchuk,
& Oksana Zabuzhko (Zephyr Press, 1994).

"One Hundred Years of Solitude, or The Importance of a Story" appeared
in *Agni Online* in July of 2016. "New Year's Letter to Oksana Zabuzhko"
appeared in *Arrowsmith Journal*, Volume VI, in January of 2020.

SELECTED POEMS

Oksana Zabuzhko

Edited by Askold Melnyczuk
with McKenzie Hurder

CONTENTS

INTRODUCTION
"Where Poetry Comes From"
(Askold Melnyczuk) / i

POEMS
Clytemnestra / 1
Cinderella / 4
Ophelia and the Mousetrap / 7
Ophelia and Gertrude / 9
Through the Looking Glass: Mrs. Merzhynsky / 12
A Commentary on the Acts of the Apostles / 15
A Kingdom of Fallen Statues / 18
Hitchhiking: A Prayer for the End of Time / 20
Turn of the Century / 24
A Toast / 27
Letter from the Summer House / 30
Diptych, 2008 / 32
Conductor of Candles / 36
A Definition of Poetry / 38

ESSAY

One Hundred Years of Solitude,
or The Importance of a Story / 43

INTERVIEW

Oksana Zabuzhko in Conversation
with McKenzie Hurder / 51

LETTER

New Year's Letter to Oksana Zabuzhko
(from Askold Melnyczuk) / 61

CONTRIBUTORS

About the Translators and Editors / 71

INTRODUCTION

"Where Poetry Comes From"
The Phenomenon of Oksana Zabuzhko

> This is what power really is: the privilege of
> ignoring anything you might find distasteful.
> — *Oksana Zabuzhko*

"Language, any language" observed the young poet Oksana Zabuzhko "is the capital love of my life" because "nothing else has the power to synthesize music and myth, two things without which the world would be a totally unlivable place." It's a credo to which Zabuzhko has remained faithful across time, even as the young poet evolved into the mature fiction writer, polemicist, and activist who is without doubt the most influential literary figure in Ukraine of the last half-century.

"You're not really a woman," reads the epigraph to Zabuzhko's *Clytemnestra*, immediately underscoring three central aspects of the poet's work. First, she's an inheritor of the Western literary tradition, grounding many of her poems in classic texts she then transforms into counter-narratives. Here Clytemnestra and Ophelia finally speak for themselves. Elsewhere, she lets us know she's read the same fairy tales, studied the same Hebrew origin stories, the same Greek myths and Roman history, along with the British classics, as have her counterparts around the world. Moreover, she's translated not only Sylvia Plath and Derek Walcott, but also the poems of contemporaries such as Marie Howe and Lucie Brock-Broido into her native Ukrainian.

Then there's the epigraph's implicit feminist subtext: Clytemnestra is indeed a woman — Helen of Troy's sister, in fact — and she's primed for battle. Initially it appears she might reject conventional male nostrums while heralding a much-needed assault on the old order. Blade in hand, awaiting her husband Agamemnon as he climbs the stairs, Clytemnestra imagines a different role for herself: "It would be a hundred times better to run off with some pilgrims,/Say, to Delphi, and become a priestess." But it's too late for that. Preparing to murder her husband, she justifies her choice: "With a single lordly gesture…/I'll outdo everything you have accomplished,/ I'll establish a new kingdom." The promised world never arises. It remains stillborn, a kingdom of statues, more monuments in civilization's graveyard. Means and ends are inseparable. "All wars," noted Ford Madox Ford, "are sexual wars."

The third note in the chord lies in the footnote to the epigraph. The line is a quote from one of Ukraine's most important writers — the playwright, poet, and novelist Larysa Kosach, who wrote under the pen name Lesia Ukrainka. No one chooses their biological parents; writers, however, get to select their literary forebearers. Zabuzhko has published a scholarly study of Lesia Ukrainka, and has edited three volumes of her collected letters. Lesia Ukrainka is as important to Ukrainian literature as Emily Dickinson to us, or George Eliot for the British. A prolific writer, she was also a political activist, a feminist at a time when the commitment carried consequences. Moreover, she herself was the daughter of a progressive father and a feminist, writer-publisher mother whom I think of as Ukraine's version of Mary Wollstonecraft and William Godwin. Lesia Ukrainka wrote her first poem, "Hope," at the age of eight in response to her aunt's arrest for protesting against the tsar. With a working knowledge of ten languages, Lesia Ukrainka also drew on Greek and Latin classics, and leaned on the Bible for plots. I have permitted myself this long aside because the fact that Lesia Ukrainka's name will mean less than nothing to anglophone readers summarizes Zabuzhko's dilemma.

In her essay "One Hundred Years of Solitude, or The Importance of a Story," first published in *Agni* in 2016, Zabuzhko observes:

> When asked, in filling out an author's questionnaire, to name which works in my genre I admire and regard as my predecessors, I choose to limit myself to *The Man Without Qualities, The Alexandria Quartet,* and *Life And Fate*, but I have to skip the Ukrainian tetralogy *Richynsky Sisters* by Iryna Wilde (1907–1982) from which I first learned how major historical events could be depicted from a woman's standpoint. My Ukrainian literary mothers aren't included in international reference books, and there's no point in trying to explain yourself by means of another unknown... Later, reading

an enthusiastic review of my novel by an American critic, I couldn't help but shudder at a sentence intended as praise: "This is especially impressive because as far as my ignorant mind was concerned, it came out of nowhere." (http://languagehat.com/the-bookshelf-the-museum-of-abandoned-secrets/). That's precisely the moment when you feel you're talking to the smiling spectators from behind a glass wall.

While a similar observation could be made by many writers from beyond the pale of the traditional Western canon, each story has its own intriguing contours. In the case of Ukraine, the glass wall has lately cracked, though not in a way that could possibly please Zabuzhko or do much to enlighten her once and future readers. A well-known writer said to me recently: "I've heard a lot about Ukrainian corruption. What about Ukrainian culture?"

○

Oksana Zabuzhko was born in 1960 in Lutsk, a town whose origins date back to the 7th century. It has ties to the Rurik dynasty — one of Europe's oldest royal houses, which endured in the region for more than 700 years. Such deep history is important in understanding the role that pride of place plays in Zabuzhko's work. Her poetry, scholarship, essays, and fiction reflect a writer determined to view her subjects in their historical contexts. Because of the way history was rewritten in the Soviet era, this has involved considerable archival excavation and led to unsettling discoveries for which Zabuzhko was better prepared than many of her peers.

During the purges of the seventies, Zabuzhko's parents, both trained philologists, may have been on the right side of history but they were on the wrong side of Soviet authorities. At the age of five, Zabuzhko found herself being babysat by a KGB agent for hours while her parents were interrogated in the next room. Surviving such an education proved excellent preparation for the years ahead.

Zabuzhko published her first poem at age ten — two years later than her heroine, Lesia Ukrainka. However, because her parents had been blacklisted, she wasn't permitted to release a book of poems until the start of the so-called "perestroika" in 1985. This period of "reconstruction," during which Moscow loosened its stranglehold on its constituent republics, and which ended with the dissolution of the Soviet Union, led to a literary renaissance: "In the decade since Gorbachev's *perestroika*, the new Ukrainian literature has enjoyed an atmosphere of freedom it hasn't known for centuries," wrote the late literary critic Solomia Pavlychko, adding: "Many writers, however, experienced that freedom well before the country declared independence in 1991. Indeed, it was largely the inner freedom felt by writers and the intelligentsia that led to independence." Writers have long played an outsized role in the evolution of Ukrainian culture. The 19th century poet Taras Shevchenko, born a serf, still enjoys the kind of iconic status which, these days, we reserve for religious figures, sports heroes, or celebrities: statues of him cast long shadows across practically every public square in the country.

I met Oksana Zabuzhko in 1990, at a poetry conference in Kyiv a year before Ukraine declared independence. It was an exhilarating period. Every city through which I passed was erupting in demonstrations. The assemblies, known locally as "manifestations," reflected the people's desire to control their own destinies. I recall standing on the stairs leading up to Lviv's Opera House early one afternoon, preparing to go in for a tour, when I heard the sounds of distant chanting. Turning around, I watched tens of thousands of protestors pour into the square in front of the Opera House. This was Tiananmen or Tahrir Square, but with a happier ending.

The following year I invited Zabuzhko to take part in a conference on "Poetry and Opposition." The event brought together an international cast of writers, including Derek Walcott, Amiri Baraka, Marjorie Agosin, Dennis Brutus, Robert Pinsky, Victor Montejo, Ha Jin, Lena Jayyusi, Bohdan Rubchak, Sam Cornish, Sven Birkerts, William Corbett, Martin Espada, Dzvinia Orlowsky, Fred Marchant, and Charles Simic. Zabuzhko subsequently returned to the US several times as a Fulbright Scholar and a writer-in-residence.

Zabuzhko reshaped the literary landscape in Ukraine with the publication of her short "American" novel, *Fieldwork in Ukrainian Sex* (1996). The book's complex prose style — sinuous Jamesian sentences scoring an intensity Plath would have seconded — with its blunt yet sophisticated sensuality, its assertively feminist slant, and a ferreting intelligence, remained a best-seller in Ukraine for over a decade, and has been translated into sixteen languages. Its subject is the trauma inflicted by totalitarian systems as it manifests in an intimate relationship. As the narrator is an intellectual, she allows herself to speculate on the nature of that trauma. A chapter from the book, translated by Halyna Hryn, was published in *Agni* in 2001. The entire novel, in Hryn's pitch-perfect rendition, finally appeared in 2011. In the last pages its heroine, who has managed to stave off the impulse to suicide, imagines herself making an announcement on the flight from the US back to Kyiv:

> "Ladies and gentlemen, we have created a wonderful world, and please accept on this occasion, sincere greetings from US Air, and from CNN, and from the CIA, and the Uruguay drug cartel, and the Romanian Securitate, and from the Central Committee of the Communist Party of China, and from the millions of killers in all the prisons of the world as well as the tens of millions still at large, and from the five thousand Sarajevo children born of rape, who will, after all, grow up some day, and — onward and upward, brave new world, and that actually is all I wanted to say, thank you for your attention, ladies and gentlemen, have a good flight."

Then, in 2009, Zabuzhko published an even more remarkable and ambitious novel, this time impressively translated by Nina Shevchuk Murray. *The Museum of Abandoned Secrets* leads readers back through the labyrinth of the last century's extreme political and personal dramas, from today's post-9/11 landscape to the Second World War. While the action in the novel takes place in Ukraine, its subject is global and its insights universal. Reading Zabuzhko on what took place in the US after September 11th, one wonders how a "stranger" can know so much about us, and can understand so clearly what has happened to our shrapneled democracy: "(A)ll talk about liberal democracy, or the Party's dictatorship, or whatever — it's all crap, forget it. The politics of today is an amalgamation of the experience of twentieth century superpowers and the experience of the marketplace of advertising. An amazingly powerful combination, if you know how to use it."

Zabuzhko the novelist is an acute and unsparing chronicler of the material world. Here's how she describes one of the dubious characters who populate this richly-peopled book: "He is capacious and amiable like a shaved, whiskerless walrus, and his breathing is a bit heavy and irregular, as happens to well-nourished men past their prime: an early shortness of breath that, if you're not used to it, might be taken for erotic arousal." And yet she does more than pin her subjects to their bodies: she also endows them with minds.

In one of the book's most illuminating passages, Daryna, the main character, meets with a former historian, now a newly minted oligarch, named Vadym. Sitting in a restaurant Vadym owns, the pair engage in the kind of wide-ranging conversation readers expect from Eastern European writers — and of a sort that's generally frowned on by Western critics, with their stifling, self-righteous fetishization of the quotidian — as though that were not the stuffing and filler of most Western fiction over the last century, as though an engagement with the realm of ideas were somehow an insult to the inescapable mundane, rather than a complementary and necessary reflection of a common human impulse, our capacity for speculating about ideas, of abstracting from immediate experience, of dreaming in words. (Isn't that what abstraction is? Language dreaming...) The pair's sprawling conversation ranges from a discussion of ice cream to imported GMO potatoes injected with scorpion genes to realpolitik. At one point, Vadym observes that "you can't draw a boundary anymore between what you call reality and what's been manufactured… realities that have been manufactured by people…" Here Vadym echoes Donald Rumsfeld's much quoted remark: "We're an empire now, and when we act, we create our own reality. And while you're studying that reality — judiciously, as you will — we'll act again, creating other new realities, which you can study too, and that's how things will sort out." Pointing out one difference between the US and Russia, Vadym observes: "The White House announced that Iraq had weapons of mass destruction — and everyone believed it. And never mind that they still haven't found those weapons — and, most likely, won't. They'll be morons, of course, if they don't; if it were the Russians, they would have planted some right away, and then no one would ever dig up what actually happened. There you have your reality…"

○

In the fall of 2013, I began receiving emails from Oksana warning me that things were heating up in Ukraine. Its president, Viktor Yanukovych, had decided not to sign an association agreement with the European Union and was on the verge of formalizing closer ties with Russia. Oksana said the threat of civil strife was real. She also mentioned that Russia had managed to influence a number of politicians across Europe, and was extending its influence into the US. This was the first I'd heard of what's come to be known as the "hybrid war" — in which propaganda plays a more important part than conventional weapons. I was at the time preoccupied with recording the damage my own country was inflicting on the Middle East. I'd traveled to Lebanon and Syria a few years before and had seen up close the grim effects of our interventions on the region's citizens, which have led to the refugee crises presently overwhelming parts of southern Europe even while we behave as if the tragedy, affecting millions and sure to be felt for generations, has nothing to do with us.

At first I dismissed her anxieties, but as the crowds in Kyiv's Independence Square (which became known as EuroMaidan on twitter) swelled, and the administration turned to violence to contain the protestors, the situation became impossible to ignore. Eventually nearly a million citizens crowded the city. President Yanukovych and his entourage were ultimately forced to flee to Russia.

The People's Rebellion succeeded in a way that similar protests throughout the Middle East had not. Zabuzhko herself was a regular on the front lines, and in the five years since she has played an active role in shoring up the freedoms for which over a hundred men and women gave their lives. Soon after the protests ended, Russia annexed Crimea and began a war on Ukraine's eastern border which has thus far left some 14,000 people dead and nearly a million displaced.

○

The glass wall Zabuzhko confronted, while cracked, stands even today. The situation recently prompted the Soviet-born

British journalist Peter Pomarantsev to observe in the *New York Review of Books Daily* that neither *London Review of Books* nor the *New York Review of Books* have ever taken notice of Ukrainian writers, despite numerous opportunities over the years.

Like most walls, this one is built of ignorance and nurtured by propaganda. A better-informed left-leaning intellectual community in the US might have been expected to support an indigenous people's efforts to preserve their culture and language. Instead, they took as fact the versions of cultural history chronicled by Russian-speaking emigres, whether the emigres themselves were from Ukraine or Russia.

This ignorance often manifested as scorn. Any number of writers I know referred to Ukraine having only a "peasant culture" — as though that in itself was somehow shameful. Or accurate. The notion of Ukraine possessing a contiguous yet distinct literature and history undermined the carefully cultivated image of a monolithic Russian culture as representative of the variety and interests of the citizens of the Soviet Union. That was never the case, and all the republics paid a heavy price for their "solidarity" with Moscow. As historian Serhii Plokhy points out: "Since the fall of the USSR, the Russian nation-building project has switched its focus to the idea of forming a single Russian nation not divided into branches and unifying the Eastern Slavs on the basis of the Russian language and culture. Ukraine has become the first testing ground for this model outside the Russian Federation."

○

"Oh my sick, shaven-headed century," Zabuzhko addresses the 20th century on the cusp — and the image feels shudderingly comprehensive. Her poems register everything from landmark moments in the writer's personal life to speculations on faith to the public trauma of Chernobyl:

> Oh yes, the neighbor's daughter
> Gave birth — a boy, a bit overdue. He had hair and teeth
> Already, and could be a mutant
> Because yesterday, only nine days old, he shouted,
> 'Turn off the sky!' He hasn't said a word since. Otherwise,
>   he's healthy.

In Zabuzhko's *Conductor of Candles*, the speaker imagines herself attending a symphony in which she alone witnesses a conductor leading an orchestra composed of lit candles: "No one sees them but me,/Flames like bullets shooting from the candelabra." She plays the conceit to its end. It's like a conversation the soul — or, consciousness — might have with itself upon emerging from Plato's cave long enough to recognize the paradox of consciousness itself.

The very word "Ukraine," often translated as "borderland," has in the past generated considerable controversy. Can a nation that describes itself as a borderland really be a country? (But what to make of the Netherlands, which recently scotched "Holland" from its self-identification?) In *A Definition of Poetry*, the poet imagines her death: "I know I will die a difficult death/

Like anyone who loves the precise music of her own body." As her soul leaves her body, the writer in her refuses to miss this rare opportunity:

> "Stop!" it screams, escaping,
> On the dazzling borderline
> Between two worlds—
> "Stop, wait.
> My God, at last.
> Look, here's where poetry comes from!"
>
> Fingers twitching for the ballpoint,
> Growing cold, becoming not mine.

The liminal, ill-defined spaces, the amorphous regions are precisely the territory where imagination flourishes. They give us room in which to shape and create ourselves as fully as our inner resources allow.

ASKOLD MELNYCZUK
MEDFORD
MARCH, 2020

POEMS

Clytemnestra

You're not really a woman.

Agamemnon's coming home.
He's climbing the stairs, the sun
Is behind him, he's clanging with brass
Like a war-bloated idol, the leather thongs
Of his armor are squeaking.
Take it off, I don't want it!
I don't want the animal smell of his mouth,
Or his hands with their black-rim red nails — those hands
Rip off my clothes as if I were a corpse on a battlefield,
And under his nails the flakes
And fuzz from the clothes and hair of the slain are rotting.
Maybe I'm not really a woman.
I don't want to scream and squirm with mortal pleasure,
Pierced by that gleaming weapon of his,
Soaked in gobs of sweat stinking
Of his regal power, trapped under his body
Trickling its sticky death-juices on me; I hate
The high-pitched bitch's whimper
That will escape my throat;
I hate the wave of languor that will embrace me
And the doughy, pitted neck above me
When I open my eyes. O son of Atreus!
That's how Troy, outstretched, writhed under you.

Your arrows target anything alive, elastic, quick —
Is it the doe? Briseis? or hot female blood
Flowing down thighs that makes you the victor,
Able to draw blood from a body like a sinless man water from a stone?
It wasn't lust or beastliness, but bestiality
To have conquered Clytemnestra and the doe and Cassandra,
Mycenae, and Troy.
Maybe I'm not really a woman.
Agamemnon's coming home, and the shadows smelling of darkness and sweat are growing longer.
I'm cold.
I'm shaking from the realization: killing is also a job!
Spinning, weaving,
Unweaving (like that woman from Ithaca), rubbing Aegisthus' rosy body (what does *he* have to do with this?)
With soothing oil —
These are pleasures for hands, occupation for hands — but not those of a queen.
They're no more noble, for instance, than fingering pockmarks.
It would be a hundred times better to run off with some pilgrims,
Say, to Delphi, and become a priestess,
To belong at every feast to every passing cripple,
To give myself up blindly to that faceless force
Without malevolence
And omnipresent — shifting, coursing, unseen...
Oh, how cold I am!

You're climbing the stairs, backlit by the sun —
Oh godlike!
More godlike, more hateful, more compelling
Is your stride up the stairs (each step weighs
One year of the Trojan war) — oh, come closer, closer...
Stiff with excitement,
Half-blinded by the black and white — this graph of shadows,
  patches of sun on the marble tiles —
I'm keeping in my sight, with the whole strength of my
  imagination,
Just this one small room
Where the curtain's burst like crimson: when you step behind it,
With a single lordly gesture
Of my hand, steady with the cold, obedient metal,
I'll outdo everything you have accomplished,
I'll establish a new kingdom,
A world without Agamemnon.

Translated by Lisa Sapinkopf

You're not really a woman: In her 1907 dramatic poem *Kassandra*, Ukrainian poet and playwright Lesia Ukrainka (1871-1913) has Cassandra speak these words to Clytemnestra when they find themselves face to face on the threshold of the palace of Mycenae upon Agamemnon's return.

CINDERELLA

Only a bitter taste remains in your mouth.
O you reclusive, tragic little fawn,
What good did it do you to have moulted
Three silver-embroidered hides,
To have slipped off, like snakeskin, the silks
Warmed with the scent of orchids and sweat,
After the waltz in which all locks
Seemed to burst for you? What of all that
When you're sitting now, blue with cold,
Back in the bleak unheated kitchen,
And the split pumpkin on the floor
Is wrinkling like a sleep-swollen face?
Or maybe it was all a dream: the ball, the blaze
Of chandeliers, the footlights, the black-mouthed halls!
You were carried by a billow of music
That seemed to italicize your every motion
In the air, as if asking: For whom
Is that spell of mine meant?
La cour was boiling like a pot of milk,
And the prince was dazzled, stopping three steps away.
Now you're sitting here. All right, go on. Throw the bark-stiff coat
Over your bare shoulders, still powdered as if cemented.
Nobody will recognize you in that kitchen –
Not prince or court, not stepmother or sisters.

In a moment your stepmother's flannel bathrobe
Will show up in the half-opened door,
And your untimely tear
Won't bring any transparency into this world.
You'll scrape their dishes,
Steep their syphilitic sheets in lye,
Rush like mad from floor to floor,
Dragging feather beds about.
You'll spread their pillowcases, wet with sighs,
And their rumpled, love-stained sheets,
X-rays of the night, in the wind
(And shut off the horizon).
This is your world.
Only the trembling membrane on your eyes
Reveals your hidden knowledge:
Somewhere in the palace your lost best shoe
Turns at dusk into a crystal slipper.
The arch springs up in a gasp, the heel is tuned like a string,
The fragile reflections glimmer, split in its blades,
And your evening-gowned silhouette streams up
From the crystal depths as though from a river bottom.
It's like TV! All the king's men
Rush in to watch the magic lantern
And admire the slipper's intricate style,
The skillful work and decoration.
Have the slipper put in a museum! In a showcase! Visitors allowed
From five o'clock (cocktails will be served) till midnight.

The prices are marked in case anyone wants a plaster copy
Of the footprint, bulletproof glass and alarm installed.
Five minutes before closing
They start to hustle the visitors away,
And the uproarious laughter and clapping of the
    subterranean hordes
Follow them, to the tolling of the clock.
You'll be the only one not to breathe a word of this,
As if your lips were frozen for good.
The newspaper's reporting on the prince's marriage
To a princess from a neighboring country — you'll tear them
    into strips
And paste them on the windows for added warmth:
Winter is almost here. You won't feel any sorrow, not you.
After all, does it really matter
Who that museum lady was?
Happy endings, soot, cinders,
The chimney shaft, the sticky mud of the court ways...
'Forgive me, please, I did my best.
My only fault was that I lost my slipper.'

Translated by Marco Carynnyk

OPHELIA AND THE MOUSETRAP

Again! How long can this go on?
Hamlet is lecturing the actors again.
Hamlet has a bald spot and a pot.
Ophelia is hiding in the gallery and smoking.
The cigarette trembles in her scrawny fingers,
Her knuckles protruding like rings,
And the classic performance is going to pieces,
Knocking our breaths out of rhythm!
> (My voice falls as if begging for water,
> My hair reeks of the kitchen,
> And even if I apply raw potatoes
> My eyes will be swollen by morning!)

What'll you have to drink, lady?
Whatever you're having.
The Ghost praises the vodka, says it's splendid.
Claudius is laughing because he's still alive,
And Hamlet is rehearsing his mousetrap.
Ophelia is smoking.
> (If only my mascara doesn't run
> And blacken the whole picture.
> Claudius enthroned. Orchestra. Fanfares.
> Hamlet is teaching the players about courage.)

Alas, my prince!
> (He bites his lip and mutters aside,
> 'To hell with your alasing!')

Made-up faces smeared by trickles of sweat,
All just mute extras.
Day after day, performance after performance,
More and more debutantes are swallowed in the crowd scenes.
Hamlet, Hamlet, something's wrong here!
It's we who are caught in the mousetrap!
Nothing's changed, as God is my witness,
Only the circles under our eyes grow darker.
O dear Lord, send me at least one soliloquy
To rend this magic circle,
Like a bottle smashed against a table
To chase the rabble away.

> (Marry a fool? I've done that.
> And a nunnery doesn't quite fit my temper.
> 'Fair Ophelia, nymph': these are just weeds
> Of words, there are no nymphs anymore.)

O dear Lord, send me at least one soliloquy
Boiling with blood, not lymph!
She stubs out her cigarette (Surgeon General's
Warning!) like someone's bent back.
Here comes the director's command:
'Ophelia, your entrance!'
She shudders.
Does she recognize the voice?

Translated by Marco Carynnyk

OPHELIA TO GERTRUDE

> KING: Gertrude, do not drink.
> *—Hamlet 5.2*

> QUEEN: Sweets to the sweet: farewell! [Scattering flowers]
> I hop'd thou shouldst have been my Hamlet's wife
> I thought thy bride-bed to have deck'd, sweet maid
> And not have strew'd thy grave.
> *—Hamlet 5.1*

Drink up your wine, Gertrude. It isn't poisoned.
It's just that the author
Couldn't be bothered with Act 6,
The one in which you will rise to your feet
And instead of sparkling with tears in the footlights
Will straighten your garments and get married —
Not out of despair, but just because.
For the third time, as for the second,
You'll be the mate of one
Who manages to tighten
A bellyband between your legs,
You royal-colored brood-mare!
You can't be stolen from your stable,
And any conqueror can seize you
As property of the crown.

So this time, I think,
You will go out to welcome Fortinbras
And with a swimmer's breast-stroke
Will cast your clothing at his feet
Like the hide of a slain lion.
(Or a slain husband?) Oh, there certainly is a queen
In Denmark! Drained by dusk,
The crystal goblet will stand
By the love-bed, where you will kneel
In the morning, doughlike,
So unlike what you were the night before,
Your lowered forehead sweating like cheese,
To give thanks to the Virgin Mary
For a womb that never grows barren
(Although your skin, to tell the truth, is becoming spotted
And a windfall of veins shows on your thighs).
Ave, regina-vagina!
Here is your realm — under the canopy
Where the curved oak legs
Creak every night till dawn.
And what difference who's kissing
This imperious mouth of yours,
Who's stamping his sealing wax
On your explosive vacuity?
You will be grand in your old age —
Stately, handsome, majestic
(Not a single superfluous motion!)
In your cloud-capped shine of grey.

Your contemporaries will swoon
From your charm: elegant in black moire,
You'll read them your memoirs
Entitled *My Son Hamlet*.
So drink calmly, Gertrude!
No harm will ever come to you.
(It was only because he was bored
That the scoundrel author did you in!)
O you unquenchable *ewig-weibliche*!
We're all your scapegoats.
And you will bury all of us
And cover everything with your lies.

Translated by Marco Carynnyk

Through the Looking Glass: Mrs Merzhynsky

In the most real of all possible worlds,
In a Kyiv that is just the same, only a little bit different
(All the cafes are on the opposite side of the street,
And the traffic runs the wrong way)
Larysa Kosach-Merzhynsky pushes a baby carriage
Along the pavement as sunlight falls through the leaves
She's pale, a bit nervous after the morning's events.
(The nanny burned the baby's cereal and has to be dismissed!)
The child churns the air with its small legs, so Mrs Merzhynsky
Stops the carriage and straightens the blanket,
Then bends over, nostrils flared, and drinks in
The warm, intoxicating fragrance of the infant's skin.
Unable to resist, she bursts into laughter
And buries her face in the frothy ticklish lace,
Then tenderly hums and clucks her tongue.
(You see, my dear Lesia, the doctor was right:
The consumption you had as a girl was simply nerves.
You'll get married, have children, and it will all pass.)

In the cafe on Prorizna (now on the other side of the street)
An angel waits, his fiery wings hidden under a grey coat.
He orders his sixth coffee. A woman in a black dress enters,
Whips off her gloves, and throws them down on the table.
The angel lifts up his eyes, then quickly looks away: she's not
   the one.

In the meanwhile Mrs Merzhynsky
Pushes the baby carriage past the cafe:
I mustn't forget the cherry-wood chips for the samovar —
Only cherry charcoal has the wonderful smell
That Serhii loves so. I must use the white tablecloth
For tea on the terrace. (Will the new cook
Manage to clean the silver?) When he comes home from work,
Still at the gate, still holding his briefcase, Mr Merzhynsky
Opens his arms as if to embrace everyone at once:
His wife and child in the wicker chair,
The nanny, who has been forgiven, and even the cook in the background.
'Lilia and her husband and Liuda Starytska will drop by later.
You know, Liuda's Ronia is older than our daughter, but she still can't walk!'

Later Mrs Merzhynsky sits by the lamp with her needlework.
The damp fragrance from the garden is more intense at dusk.
A neighbor's window slams; someone is calling the children home.
And then a cry rings out, probably from the Jewish quarter: 'Miriam!'
(The hills echo, 'Miriam! Miriam!') Startled,
Mrs Merzhynsky pricks her finger with the needle.
'What is it, dear?' 'It's nothing.' The glistening ruby
On her fingertip dries as a rusty spot on the cambric handkerchief.
Miriam, Miriam. O Lord. No, I can't remember.

'You're simply tired'; he kisses her palm. 'Isn't it time to go
   to bed?'
(She throws her arms around his neck with a sigh and a shiver.)
In the cafe on Prorizna (now on the other side of the street) the
   angel
Orders his twelfth coffee. No one in sight. The clock
Strikes twelve — it must be midnight. Happy women
Are asleep, exhausted by their loving labors. Mrs Merzhynsky
Lies motionless on her back beside her sleeping husband.
Her eyes, dry but burning as if after a long cry,
Are open wide as she stares into the empty night.

Translated by Virlana Tkacz and Wanda Phipps

Larysa Kosach-Merzhynsky: The real name of Lesia Ukrainka. She contracted tuberculosis as a child and was sickly most of her life. She was in love with Serhii Merzhynsky, who died of TB in 1901. In 1907 she married Klyment Kvitka, but they were not happy and had no children.

A woman in a black dress: Lesia Ukrainka is usually portrayed in black, and is known to have been high-strung.

Liuda Starytska: The writer Liudmyla Starytska-Cherniakhivska was a friend of the Kosach family.

Miriam: The central figure in Lesia Ukrainka's play *A Woman Obsessed*, which she wrote as Serhii Merzhynsky was dying. The play's subject is Miriam's boundless love for the Messiah, which prevents her from being able to forgive his enemies.

A Commentary on the Acts of the Apostles

So why are you standing here, Peter?
The sentries have disappeared around the corner,
And only the roar of the crowd can be heard from the vicar's palace.
What difference, in the end, whether he was God or not?
The rub is somewhere else, though even Pilate doesn't know where.
The crowd is growing. With hoarse shrieks and beer stench
People crawl from their dark burrows to Golgotha.
A provincial actor, booed off stage by a cock three times in a row,
You stand still, your face cloaked in the vulgar heathen manner,
Your fingers rough and stumpy, your skin tanned by stinking fish.
Does the apostolic name really suit Simon the fisherman?
Of course, you're not the one who's ready to take thirty pieces of silver,
But neither are you the one who's prepared to be crucified for his people.
And for whom should I crucify myself, God Almighty?
My tattered net brings up only slime and silt.
Oh, leave me alone, everybody.
I *do not know* this man.
I don't owe anything to anyone,
And least of all to him.

Yes, I was with him. Through my tears, crushed by the rabble,
I gazed ecstatically, and listened, and wept hosannahs. What
 a fool!
Why not ask instead: Teacher, what's your teaching to them?
Just feed them five loaves of bread and change water into wine!
Oh, and some tricks, too. Raising the dead,
Swallowing fire, pacing on a knife blade: that'll hit the mark.
But how can I walk on water as if it were dry land
When my faith has been corroded for so many years?
Oh, this roar from the crowd and these shameless moist
Black olives under Magdalene's curved lashes
Here even death is acting: the hero will be resurrected
And will emerge in his glory to accept the audience's applause.
Every detail has been thought of, the script is in its final draft:
To rake up scads of people's hearts like loose change.
The money-changers thrown out of the temple, we've taken
 their places.
I am your disciple, Jesus. Perhaps the last zealot.
I feared such a finale much more than Golgotha.
And amidst the changing teachings and prophets (O endless
 epoch!),
Amidst the spectred chapels and torture chambers, the pulp of
 dark ages,
Only the man who renounced you three times before the dawn
 is real.
Noon is near, and he's still standing.
So here you are, Peter, filling half the horizon as you stand here.

Doesn't the multitude of earthly laments reach you?
The gate of paradise is locked behind him,
And his hammy fist is clenching rusty keys.

Translated by Marco Carynnyk

A Kingdom of Fallen Statues

Just as children scrawl self-portraits
With two figures — mom and dad —
Grasping them by their unsteady stick-hands,
I'm drawing on the windowpane
A kingdom of fallen statues —
And the outlines, delicate and fine, are wavering.
In the kingdom of fallen statues all gates stand open;
Even marauders no longer walk on the grass
That seems to have shot to full height in a flash.
Non-existent temples
And, yes, non-existent dramas —
But how real, O God, how very much alive they are…
Gilding and lapis flake like skin
From the leprous faces of princes and saints.
And, seated on tombstones or perhaps on column stumps,
Black-hooded gravediggers roll cigarettes in yellowed verse.
Don Quixote's shield lies somewhere,
Somewhere Casanova's cloak was tossed,
Somewhere stands the tent in which Khmelnytsky hosted
Europe's envoys.
In the kingdom of fallen statues you can hear a language
Of words still warm but no longer learned.
I'm drawing it all: everything that ever vanished, or will;
I peer into my picture as into ripples on water:
Triumphant Nike's head

Is lying somewhere in the grass.
I'll draw it — and then
I'll place the period.

Translated by Lisa Sapinkopf

Hitchhiking: A Prayer for the End of Time

Hail Mary, full of grace, the Lord is with thee — if he's here at all, that is, if he hasn't shut his eyes and ears against us: 'Here's another fine mess I've gotten myself into,' said the child and, shaking its head, refused to be born (insert statistics about the increase in infant mortality rates here); Mary, you get off the Greyhound amid the endless fields, just like in the other world, of Nebraska, or maybe Iowa, I watch you from my window, the only other white person on the bus is sleeping on my shoulder, a grey face with a reddish three-day growth and prominent blue ropes of veins on thin asthenic arms — how did it turn out that we, the only two white people, ended up side by side?

(Scene from a horror movie: a corpse, drowned in a giant aquarium; pressed to the glass, a face with wide eyes now popping like fisheyes turns pale — a face whose soul has left it, blowing upward in gentle bubbles — is that how you see me, Mary?)

The sound, where's that sound from, like dozens of doors creaking one after the other, high-pitched, like a plucked bow — someone gets off, someone else gets on, hey, folks, why don't you grease it?

Mary Mary Rodriguez, or maybe Maria Alvarez, your skin like buckwheat honey flashing the driver a toothy goodbye, handbag tossed over a round shoulder — how will you cross the field, alone, the endless field, like in the other world? Though they say they're building in the other world, block by block, concrete walls dripping with graffiti, open garbage cans — Bronx, Harlem, Borshchahivka, Vidradnyi — and kids as pale as spud roots pluck eyeballs from stray cats (ba-ba-bam! — the beat of rap from headphones). An old man shuffles out of the house on the corner and gives us the finger.

Maria, we invented this world — the melting white flesh turning into bluish ice-cream on the slowly warming planet, a damned race with bad blood in its veins, like my neighbor's, for instance (he's moved — let the poor bastard sleep): conquistadors, Vikings, crusaders, pirate assaults and Cossack bread, skin that pales in an iron cell of armour, and even our yellow Slavic butter — anyone who wanted to could spread us on our black soil and make himself a sandwich — even it stinks from who knows what. In the holds of what slave ships was your blood carried overseas, Mary? Standing at the side of the road, you swell before my eyes, filled with the juices of light (in my sight, in the trembling of my tear), your pregnancy near term, neat as a bud, while we've infected half of Africa with Aids — and now we're dying (see graph showing the decrease in the birth rate for European nations). After that turn, where the bus is now heading, in the third millennium, we're simply not around.

I'm cold, Mary, we're spilled milk, and I feel how wave on wave of fever burns through me, clearing everything, leaving only the body, a thin-skinned vessel coated with scum — pray for us, Mary. Two white people in a bus at the end of time, a drug addict and a keeper of a half-dead language — tonight I dreamed I was squeezing my own barren breasts like a pimple and a black pearl of oil oozed from the left nipple — oh, call out the angels, call out the medical orderlies, call the Lord on the hotline, and let someone save us. The bus starts, you stand with your back to oncoming traffic, your round shoulders, round butt, skin the color of buckwheat honey, you raise your hand slowly, moving as if the air were molasses: you're a hitchhiker, an intercontinental tumbleweed — from where? From the colored neighborhoods of Chicago? Aren't you from Sacramento Street, didn't your brothers beat a white student there last night, heels stomping his groin?

Blessed art Thou among women, and blessed be the fruit of Thy womb, and this sound, this squeaking — like the door opening and closing, letting someone off — why didn't I guess sooner, that's just them sharpening their knives!

Sancta Maria, Mater Dei, ora pro nobis...

My neighbor finally lifts his head, opens his eyes, smiles weakly — and I see (who does he remind me of, with his wan face, his sharp features and cracked lips, and three days' growth?) how, as from the tungsten filament inside a lamp, a faint glow seeps out around his head. I begin to cry, deeper and deeper, as though I wanted to get it over with once and for all, while the retarded creature looks on, quiet, feeble, and gentle, and now

I'm crying aloud, and a Voice — without words and without speech — comes from within as the clap of a bell to my skull, to this heated glass ball on the verge of splitting, and swaying it, says: Peace be with thee, sister.

A turn, and the Greyhound heads into the tunnel.

Translated by Askold Melnyczuk

Bronx, Harlem, Borshchahivka, Vidradnyi: Borshchahivka and Vidradnyi are working-class districts in Kyiv.

Turn of the Century

You won't feel it right away, only after summer's gone.
They're closing down the cafes and bringing in the tables
    from the terraces.
The air is hissing out of this century as from a rubber ball,
While the coming one is inflating, unnoticed, already not ours.
Our century, brief as an exhalation:
Another minute, and amidst the ashen snows
Your city will have stiffened
Into a series of souvenir postcards
Of parks and streets in which you've never set foot.
Who then will gather our ailing, obscure voices
And revive the sound of our city on the warm hills,
While the sky gapes empty where cathedrals stood for ages,
And hordes of tourists pass, indifferent as their camera lenses?

O cruel century, launched with wars and butcheries!
We've barely had a chance to forget the past —
And already some 747 is crashing on our heads from the sky,
Its wrenched wing sagging, bloodied.
O mortal century of ours!
Anyone afflicted with it, as though with youth,
Will feel its hand on his shoulder for a lifetime.
The year when (according to the timetable) I'll turn forty,
The iron gates will slam shut on this century,
And the key will splash into the water.

O my sick, my shaven-headed century!

How quickly, how unheard you'll be tucked away in the hospital!

Yet we learned, as children, to shuck

The essence from your newsreels like chocolates from foil,

We could see while still in the womb,

Were ready for anything while in the cradle.

On the charred stumps of families exterminated to the last soul,

We were conceived by rehabilitated parents

Who pumped the blue oxygen of hope into our veins.

We followed in their footsteps.

We were born lucky, pure:

We've never shot anyone in the back, nor been shot in the face.

Why, then, the laboured breathing of this city on the hills

As though it were sketched with a harsh, hasty pencil?

We were never shelled in trenches with fire, muck, and curses,

The pencil never fell from our bloodless, feeble grasp —

It's just that, for some reason, they cancelled our classes in aesthetics,

Marched us to the enlisting office,

And gave us draft cards along with our diplomas.

We clinked through our youth with its small change of words,

Frittered love away God knows with whom or where,

All the while recalling, with the unconscious memory of our insatiable bodies,

How Afghan sands sprout from Kyiv blood.

So, with my glazed, frozen eyes aimed at tomorrow,

I cry out to all of you, as if tapping Morse code on a wall:
Write down, oh, please write down
This city of ours, the most beautiful on earth,
Gnawed like lips in pain,
Cast in this dense century as though in amber!
Then, let it be not with our names, but with our birthdates
That we head into the looming century.
Age will keep us going — and we'll continue our story:
After our fortieth birthday, before, as long as we're alive.

Translated by Lisa Sapinkopf

A Toast

I drink to the only brotherhood I know:
To an itinerant theatre, to a village band on a country road,
To poets reading to each other in a room with drawn curtains,
To the artists' studios on Andriivsky Uzviz.
I drink to you, my poisoned-blood brothers, and especially to you, sisters,
To the permanent neuroses you can't get by without,
To your doubts layered over a secret: the grass won't grow without you.
I drink to those of you I'll never hear of, nor they of me,
To all the fingers wrung in the woods of the keys, to the windfall of drafts,
To the post-rehearsal blood on the flutist's lips, to the unnamed
And unrealized conception with a single moment of freedom
Caught within it, to the sweat in the gyms, to the drenched ballet tights
Actors shrug off like moulted skins,
To the canvases coated with dried stains as if with the vomit of exhaustion
To lively faces turned into satyrs' masks on the night of failure, when the decision to destroy the manuscript is made,
To the tears of impotence, to the dents of fingernails on unclutched palms,
To the alcohol-burnt blackholes in brains, to the syncopes

Of the desperate muscle thrusting against the left breast, near
   to tearing it through.
I drink to all the defeats that wash the shine from your eyes,
Sleep from your nights, the most beloved woman (or man)
   from your lives,
To your painful envy of the talent of your tribe,
And to the fact that no one will ever know its true value as
   you do.
I drink to the luminous insatiability that sucks you from inside,
Whistling in your bone hollows and choking on itself,
To your unending solitude in a world that wasn't made for you
(And it's good that it wasn't, for otherwise what would it be
   good for?).
I drink to your not knowing whether this world wants to be
   named,
Wants to be caught in your golden nets of notes, images,
   chiaroscuros.
I drink to your outcast's lot, you martyrs without holiness
(And, frankly, perhaps without faith?),
To the ease you break your toys with, to the innocence of your
   stripping,
To the predacious ecstasy of your chasing the falling star:
   seek it!
And to your fickleness, which is in fact an immunity to
   everything
That diverts you from your pursuit as a smell distracts a hound.
And to your secret indifference to the completed piece:
   no matter

Whether it's used to stuff the archives or flood the market.
I drink to your indefatigable marathon gropings, to all the weeks
You're failures, and to the hours you're godlike.
To you, then, you community of those branded before conception
With the adolescent hunch that life's holding out on you,
I drink, and smash my glass, and here assert
This is the only lasting love I know on this planet.

Translated by Marco Carynnyk

Andriivsky Uzviz: The street in Kyiv where most of the art galleries and studios are located.

LETTER FROM THE SUMMER HOUSE

Dear ———— ,

The land's rusty again.
Acid rain: our blackened cucumber vines
Jut from the earth like scorched wire.
And I'm not sure about the orchard this year.
It needs a good cleaning up,
But I'm scared of those trees.
When I walk
Among them, it feels like I'm going to step
On some carcass rotting in the tall grass,
Something crawling with worms, something smiling
Sickly in the hot sun.
And I get nervous over the most innocent sounds:
The day before yesterday, in the thicket, meowing,
The monotonous creaking of a tree,
The suppressed cackling of geese — all constantly
Straining for the same note.
Do you remember
That dry elm, the one lightning turned
Into a giant charred bone last summer?
Sometimes I think it lords
Over the whole garden, infecting everything with rabid madness.
How do mad trees act?
Maybe they run amok like derailed streetcars.

Anyway, I keep an axe by the bed, just in case.
At least the butterflies are mating: we'll have
Caterpillars soon. Oh yes, the neighbor's daughter
Gave birth — a boy, a bit overdue. He had hair and teeth
Already, and could be a mutant
Because yesterday, only nine days old, he shouted,
'Turn off the sky!' He hasn't said a word since. Otherwise, he's healthy.
So, there it is. If you can get away
For the weekend, bring me something to read
In a language I don't speak.
The ones I call mine are exhausted.

Kisses, love, O.

Translated by Douglas Burnet Smith

Diptych, 2008

I

You said to love them, Lord,
this red light beating my lashes
this mob of Boschian mugs hurling their stones at You
dragging from the depths of withered souls
the darkest curses under heaven:
"Crucify him! Crucify him!" rips from their throats.
Rattling like the metro, from the underground tunnel of time
(hear the wagons knocking along the tracks)—
comes an echo: "Sig heil! Sig heil!"
Eyes shut,
arms out
fists clenched.
These are Your people, Lord.
See: they haven't changed:
amphitheaters, colosseums,
bestiaries,
the smell of human flesh burning on the plazas of Madrid,
they're the ones carrying kindling for an auto-da-fe
nostrils flare inhaling whiffs of a heretic's bones
(the executioner draws down his red mask,
the technician focuses the camera lens on his eyes,
a centurion adjusts his belt buckle…).

And these are my people, Lord,
exiting the train on wobbly legs
falling, drunk on their first sips of freedom,
trembling, they rise, gather in crowds,
their cloudy gaze scans the horizon for a shepherd,
an inquisitor, a caesar, a centurion—
whoever tells them: "Come, kneel before me—
and free yourselves of your selves!"
Out they pour, muscles stiffening,
hands probing for stones,
eyes half-lidded, blood pulsing,
from their starved throats
rises the same, two-thousand year old
rhythmic growl.

These are Your people, Lord.
Send them your Son again.
Come, Lord:
They're ready.

II

8/8/2008 — the start of the Russian-Georgian war

History, you bitch,
again you've got me by the throat,
again you've shaken my soul,

again you send my thoughts
down a tunnel echoing with the cry:
"*No passaran!* They will not pass!"—
blocking the view
with the gray cobblestones of the morning news,
internet whore, like after a shelling
again you color the world in two shades of the spectrum—
the blood sacrifice—red,
                        and the dirt gray of evil…
Again sleepless nights scythe me down
like a field across which armies march
and again I'm climbing into a tank,
knocking on armor, turning wheels
turning words into petitions and appeals
to keep it from happening:
No passaran! They will not pass!

History, bitch, damn you—
they pass, they always pass:
over the corpses of hope,
trampling dreams—
if not this way, then that, if not straight, then sideways, or crabwise,
maneuvering, capturing territories
one by one, pushing in
through cracks and fissures,
through the sealed and the open,
turning all to ruin, covered in husks

of lives chewed up and spat out
                          faith shredded…
So that's why I'll stand
here on this narrow ledge in full armor
including a gas mask,
and wail like a banshee "They will not pass!"
if only to signal
(an ironic point of light on a map of a world without borders)
that at least here, at this little dot on the map
I can keep vigil
with sixty kg of my living body
and maybe, perhaps,
they really will not
be able to pass?

Translated by Askold Melnyczuk

Conductor of Candles

Conductor of candles! Pupils shimmer with reflections…
Black web of shadows, break apart for an instant —
Yes, for just the simple gesture with which he tears off his gloves
I'd accept even more than my earthly travails!
Conductor of candles! Your arms, all sinews and veins,
Are bared nearly to the shoulders in the unsteady light.
I can feel all the glib, sticky smiles peel away from my face
As fingers rub the melted residue of candles.
The stage lights up with a parching glow,
Your silhouette is distinct, indelible, even through closed lids,
Conductor of candles! No one sees them but me,
Flames like bullets shooting from the candelabra
In the seat next to mine a bearded oaf is snoring.
In front of me plump dresses exhale perfume.
Conductor of candles! No one hears you but me
In this hall where people doze their lives away.
What's the point of this, maestro? Who needs it?
Look around —we're alone in this hall!
'The first candle stinks!
What this orchestra of yours needs is a couple of good sparklers!'
Voices rustle in the dark like banknotes.
I peer without blinking into the candles' golden pupils.
Conductor of candles! I know the charred wicks of your fingers
Will flare up at any moment into petals of living fire!

Oh, how people will leap from their chairs, squeaking and shrieking,
When the splash of sparks rends the curtain of darkness,
When you burst to the ceiling like a living torch,
Shedding furious fireworks on their sleepy faces!
And when your still-warm ashes have burned into stagnant brains
(My God, for whom, before whom, have you burned?)
I will shape a thin candle from the pure, prescient wax,
Walk down the empty aisle and climb to the stage...
I'll tear off my gloves —
The black web of shadows will break apart for an instant —
And I'll step up to your podium as conductor of the last candle,
Until the moment I'm replaced.

Translated by Lisa Sapinkopf

A Definition of Poetry

I know I'll die a difficult death —
Like anyone who loves the precise music of her own body,
Who knows how to force it through the gaps in fear
As through a needle's eye,
Who has danced a lifetime with the body — every move
Of shoulders, back, and thighs
Shimmering with mystery, like a Sanskrit word.
Muscles playing under the skin,
Like fish in a nocturnal pool.
Thank you, Lord, for giving us bodies.
When I die, tell the carpenters
To take down the rafters and ceiling
(They say my great-grandfather, a sorcerer, got out this way).
When my body softens with moisture,
The bloated soul, dark and bulging,
Will strain
Like a blue vein in a boiled egg-white,
And the body will ripple with spasms.
Like the blanket a sick man wrestles off
Because it's hot…
And the soul will rise to break through
The press of flesh, curse of gravity.
The Cosmos
Above the black well of the room
Will suck on its galactic tube

Heaven breaking in a blistering starfall
And draw the soul up, trembling like a sheet of paper —
My young soul —
The color of wet grass —
To freedom — then
"Stop!" it screams, escaping,
On the dazzling borderline
Between two worlds —
'Stop, wait.
My God, at last.
Look, here's where poetry comes from!'

Fingers twitching for the ballpoint,
Growing cold, becoming not mine.

Translated by Michael M. Naydan and Askold Melnyczuk

ESSAY

One Hundred Years of Solitude, or The Importance of a Story

"Within the past few months, Ukraina, a nation unknown to the West, has come into the forefront of the world's attention. Most people, I think, are prepared to say that they know little or nothing about it. For this deficiency in knowledge they need not blame themselves. There are good reasons for it. The suppressors of Ukraina took care that she be unknown; they indeed denied that she even existed. It would be difficult to imagine anything more reprehensible than this silencing of a nation which by ancient right belongs to the European family of nations. But uncontrollable events have now brought Ukraina into the international arena."

These words are not from today's media: the quotation is seventy-five years old. It belongs to British journalist Lancelot Lawton. During the 1930s, with the smog of totalitarianism thickening over Europe, Lawton was trying to open the eyes of the British public to the importance of the "Ukrainian question" in the forthcoming and unavoidable (as he wisely foresaw) battles in Eastern Europe. Though he delivered a special address on the issue in the House of Commons, Lawton's message passed unheard. The West completely missed his "Ukrainian lesson" and crossed Ukraine off its list for many decades. Nor did the reappearance of the country on the political map in 1991 help to make it more recognizable: there is simply no room for Ukraine's story in the Western narrative as long as the "The Soviet Story" (to use the title of Edvins Snore's famous film) goes unrevised.

When history's lessons are overlooked, it sends its careless students back to the classroom to retake the exams they once failed. And that's exactly where we are now — with our unlearned lessons from the twentieth century, and our incapacity to recognize in what we watch and hear in today's news from troublesome regions (of which, notably, there are more and more!) a revival — or, more than once, a linear continuation — of the same historical plots that for decades have been deleted from our cultural memory. We face them blind and deaf, unable to grasp what's going on.

It's a big temptation for a writer to play with counterfactual history, to re-plot events as if some big moment had turned out differently. For years my personal obsession — quite a masochistic one, I have to admit — has been to picture a world in which the Ukrainian People's Republic of 1918-1920 didn't collapse under the Bolshevik invasion, and Ukraine, along with Poland and Finland, managed to preserve its national independence and cultural identity, rather than transforming into the drowned Atlantis of the European subconscious. One thing can be said for sure: the world would've been a different place — and, in all likelihood, a better one. A lost country is, after all, more substantial than Bradbury's butterfly, and the multiple lacunae produced in the contemporary Western mind, with all things Ukrainian missing from it, remind me of a CT scan of a brain struck with atherosclerosis: the risk of developing stroke is extremely high. The problem is, to see "the holes in the picture" one has to be Ukrainian. And Ukrainians aren't particularly good at communication. For decades it's keeping silent, not speaking, that our survival instincts have taught us.

One hundred years of our solitude — of our cultural non-existence, in the view of the outside world — has left my generation of writers with a sense of irreparable damage. Even when appearing now on the international stage, we are doomed to remain, at best, half-understood, like tongue-tied cripples, because the cultural context we belong to remains invisible to the non-Ukrainian public. When asked to name in the Amazon authors' questionnaire which works in my genre I admire and envision as my predecessors, I choose to limit myself to *The Man Without Qualities*, *The Alexandria Quartet*, and *Life And Fate*, but I have to skip the Ukrainian tetralogy *Richynsky Sisters* by Iryna Wilde (1907–1982) from which I first learned how major historical events could be depicted from a woman's standpoint. My Ukrainian literary mothers aren't included in international reference books, and there's no point in trying to explain yourself by means of another unknown…

Later, reading an enthusiastic review of my novel by an American critic, I couldn't help but shudder at the seemingly praising lines: "This is especially impressive because as far as my ignorant mind was concerned, it came out of nowhere" (http://languagehat.com/the-bookshelf-the-museum-of-abandoned-secrets/). That's precisely the moment when you feel you're talking to the smiling spectators from behind a glass wall.

Behind this wall, Russian troops came to kill us in full view of the whole world, the same way they did a hundred years ago. And the world watched, stupefied and lost in guesses: shouldn't there be a rationale justifying, at least partly, such behavior? After all, the Russian, a.k.a. Soviet, story sounds familiar, and that story drags a whole set of instantly identifiable images with it. On the Ukrainian part there's nothing in the least comparable… and the storyteller takes all — no matter whether his story is true or a pack of lies.

That's how we have come to learn that for a free nation the strategy of survival is in fact to speak, not to keep silent. Today's Ukrainian literature is struggling to put into words the most burning human material possible: the reality of war. And it's in this struggle that our century-old Atlantis, once drowned in blood, is suddenly resurfacing for us in all its painful, tragic beauty — its prophets and martyrs, dead geniuses and forgotten heroes, giving new dimension to the close-ups of history now appearing before us at accelerated speed, calling for new accounts and new portrayals. It looks as if, rediscovering their identity in the war of independence, Ukrainians have finally discovered how much they have to tell the world.

If only, this time, the world will listen.

INTERVIEW

Oksana Zabuzhko In conversation with McKenzie Hurder

At an awards ceremony at my college graduation, the dean read a brief note about each student, mentioning her accomplishments and future plans. When it was my turn, the dean noted that I was in the process of applying for a Fulbright Scholarship to research contemporary Ukrainian literature. Afterwards, a Ukrainian man who had attended the ceremony stopped me in the university foyer between two sets of automatic sliding glass doors to ask me if I was Ukrainian, or if my family could trace their heritage back to Ukraine, and if not, where in the world did this interest possibly come from? This question became one I was asked frequently as I shared my interests with my former professors and started to attend public lectures at the Harvard Ukrainian Research Institute. It seemed few people without direct links to Ukraine were reading Ukrainian literature.

I found Oksana Zabuzhko's work via a very fortunate google search. I knew a fair amount about English and American writers from reading them my whole life. I was also acquainted with a number of canonical works from Germany, France, and Czechia, as well as a few Russian poems that had been covered in my university courses. I wondered why I had never read any writing from Ukraine. I immediately ordered — and devoured — *Fieldwork in Ukrainian Sex*, an intensely intimate confessional that explores the intersection of national and gender identity. I became simultaneously enthralled and frustrated: some themes were familiar to me, like the struggles that come with living as a brutally independent woman in a patriarchal society, while others eluded me, like the mixed feelings that come with being fiercely proud of one's country and feeling largely invisible because of it. It isn't that the book failed to articulate this phenomenon; rather, I didn't know enough about Ukraine's singular history to grasp the source of Zabuzhko's strong feelings. To understand the context for Zabuzhko's work, and to untangle the mysteries of these unfamiliar themes, I undertook the task of learning as much as I could about Ukrainian history, politics, and culture, at the same time as I immersed myself in as much of Zabuzhko's work as I could find.

Ironically, as I persisted in this research, Ukraine suddenly became a trending topic in American news. Everything my friends and family knew about Ukraine came from sensationalized media outlets in the context of an American scandal, and I began to witness and understand the complexity and importance of Zabuzhko's work. It is an exciting opportunity to be part of the release of her selected poems in translation. Her work continues to speak to a new generation of women writers (myself included). It seems profoundly important that this incredibly rich literature, with its feminist stance coming from

Ukraine today, be made available to a new English-speaking audience. The conversation about women's rights and their evolving rule in our society is, after all, an international one. In the course of my reading, I've come to admire Oksana Zabuzhko for her writing, feminism, and political activism, and it is my great honor to have had the opportunity to interview her.

McKenzie Hurder
Boston, MA
February, 2020

○

McKenzie Hurder

A majority of these selected poems were initially written and published in the 90's. With the political and social changes that have taken place in Ukraine during the last 30 years, do you relate to these poems differently now? Do you feel your newer poems handle themes of national identity and womanhood differently, and if so, in what ways?

Oksana Zabuzhko

It's not the matter of my changing views or feelings (I don't think I've changed much in this regard), but simply of aging, I suspect — of a changing time perception. I write poems less now, because of a special kind of laziness I've started developing since I turned 50: Why bother yourself producing another poem in the world already flooded with books, if someone else has already expressed similar feelings in her own words? Why not limit yourself to what you know you still must tell, for no one else would do it for you, and the sand in your hourglass is rushing? And, yes, like every author, I prefer my mature poems to my early ones — they are more laconic, less garrulous (more knowledgeable, less emotional), but, most importantly, they are of my current age.

McKenzie Hurder

As a new generation of women Ukrainian poets begin to write, do you feel their handling of national identity and womanhood in their own work is similar to your own? In what ways do you see the influence of your work on theirs?

Oksana Zabuzhko

I always feel uneasy when I have to admit my role of a "literary matriarch" (even though in one of my poems, written at 37, I claimed an ambition to be one, "to guard someone younger" with my text, and poems do come true in the long run, this I can now say for sure!). Ukrainian poetry now boasts a constellation of amazingly good women poets in their 30s, who may have really benefited from "growing up in my shade" (critics know about this more than I do), but when I come to read at some international festival along with, say, Iryna Tsilyk and Katya Kalytko, I don't feel like a mother goose with daughters — I feel like we're equal, and a team, all writing with the same language and the same "nerve," the only difference being that such a strong "girls' team" was impossible to imagine in my literature when I was their age…

Mᶜ Kenzie Hurder

One of the most brilliant aspects of your poems is their ability to be personal and confessional in the same breath that they encapsulate a much larger history and a more universal experience. Is this something you consciously think about in the beginning stages of writing? Why do you feel your writing has connected with readers across borders and generations?

Oksana Zabuzhko

Thank you for this observation, I treasure it. It's always been my ambition, both in poetry and in prose, to find a universe of senses in a shadow under a collar bone — deep in my heart I secretly believe that's what literature is for. I never write "consciously," though, and would've never been able to write, say, a detective novel, for I refuse to grasp what can drive you through 300 pages if all this time you knew in advance who killed a girl in Chapter One. What is the point to write if not to find out how the things were? For me, writing is moving in the dark (in prose, in the fog), following words that gradually turn into lights — and the best pleasure of writing is to see how things discover themselves, when approached "under a proper angle." It's like archeology, only you hunt for the meaning of life, and when you're fully engaged into it, your reader will be engaged, too, no matter language and generation boundaries.

McKenzie Hurder

Are the reactions from American readers, scholars, and press different from reactions in Ukraine? Do you feel Western readers are more likely to misinterpret your work, or miss the point entirely?

Oksana Zabuzhko

Virginia Woolf had separated in her diaries the pleasure of writing from the pleasure of being read, and within the latter I would separate "the pleasure of being translated." Every act of reading is a dialogue, every book (or piece) has as many versions as it has readers. And when you read reviews of your work in translation, the most interesting part is not what it tells you about your work (after all, the work is your past, for how long can you stay tuned to what reactions it awakes in people?) — but what it tells you about the other, foreign culture. It's really an exciting, and inexhaustible subject — to explore cultures through their "reflections" in your work (like in a fairy tale: tell me what you saw in this lake, and I'll tell you who you are). I don't believe there's a thing like a "proper interpretation" of a piece of literature — if it serves as a clue to open in a reader some wells of her own thoughts/imagination/memories/emotions, previously closed, it's the best of what literature can do, for that's what it is for: to connect people, notwithstanding any borders in time or space.

LETTER

New Year's Letter to Oksana Zabuzhko
from Askold Melnyczuk

My Dear O,

I began this letter a month ago, a few days after our president was impeached. The moment was historic, but it didn't feel that way. Maybe that's because the world's on fire: Paris was shut down for months by strikes; the rainforests keep burning along with vast stretches of California and Australia; there have been protests in Hong Kong, Santiago, and Caracas, not to mention in Kabul, Cairo, Beirut, Tehran, New Delhi, Bogota, and Baghdad. Ukraine is a soccer ball kicked around by parties who care only about scoring goals. These days, newspapers spare little room for the Syrians, Tibetans, Uighurs, Rohingya, or the Kurds. Occasional stories about these tragic places appear fleetingly, like trees glimpsed along a highway down which you're hurtling full speed, heading who knows where?

I began my letter and put it aside repeatedly. There's too much to say and every day the headlines offer fresh jolts. I've also written little about our contemporary political situation in part because so much of what I think gets voiced already across a thousand platforms. I keep remembering lines from a poem by my old professor, the wonderful poet Ira Sadoff: "I read the papers and weep./ I give the finger to the president." Yes, both.

At the same time, as my country prepares for elections, one needs to clarify one's thoughts and hopes.

I know what you did to your corrupt president when he wouldn't leave: you chased him out. He didn't go peacefully, though. You, I know, are still coming to terms with the trauma of those days out on the streets of Kyiv, fires burning, the Berkut shooting protestors from rooftops. Blood was spilled. I hope, and expect, we'll manage to avoid that. You "won" that battle — and yet the war goes on. Everywhere, perpetual war. As my friend Leila, a political scientist, pointed out, we've entered a world devoid of all principles: winning is everything. Principles are inconveniences, encumbrances, to be discarded like rinds.

The subversion of all values is everywhere. Consider the case of the Sackler family, whose pharmaceutical company promoted the abuse of addictive opioids even as the family purchased respectability by patronizing the arts at the highest cultural levels, at the Metropolitan Museum, at Harvard, at Yale. Several of the company's founders were themselves physicians who had taken an oath to "do no harm." The institutions receiving their money never asked where it came from, and never allowed themselves to consider that what they were doing was tantamount to money laundering. Hundreds of thousands of deaths are directly linked to the family's accumulation of billions, several billion of which they are now trying to shield from the lawsuits being brought by attorneys-general around the country. And they are just one case among thousands dramatizing what happens when the ethos of money and winning at any cost become the rule of the land. We could as easily consider the Koch brothers, the circle surrounding Jeffrey Epstein, and of course, our president.

Do you remember an observation made by Albert Camus, a writer we both love, in his magnificent, still relevant book, *The Rebel*? The central problem of the 19th century, he wrote, was how to live in a world abandoned by grace. With God gone missing, the solution then turned on humans creating their own earthly paradise, a utopia founded on the principle of justice. But justice according to whom? Lenin? Hitler? By the middle of the 20th century the question became: how do we live in a world ruled by neither grace nor justice?

Events have already provided the answer. Into the vacuum marched the will to power: power not even nominally in service of grace or justice, but rather as an absolute value in and of itself. This is certainly not the first time in history power for its own sake held sway over the human imagination: "Might makes right" describes the relation between polities in "a state of nature." That ethos appeared to have lost credibility after the devastations of the Second World War. The evolution of international institutions such as the UN and the EU, seemed to indicate that humanity had recognized its common stake in mutual well-being. Disasters teach lessons too soon forgotten.

Unlike its predecessors, grace and justice, power in service of itself appears unwilling to yield the floor. Even formulating the next question is difficult. What might arise once we admit that not grace, not justice, not even the will to power have, will, or can succeed in bringing the social forces tearing us apart into some kind of equilibrium? Yet until we do imagine it, power and the pursuit of it will seem like the only game in town.

Power is the subject of our oldest literature. Long before Foucault, Homer's *Iliad* chronicled power's fluidity. In her essay "Poem of Force" Simone Weil analyzes the ways in which everyone in Homer's poem abuses power in the brief moments they appear to possess it, never realizing it is power that possesses them. And once they overstep, retribution is certain:

> This retribution, which has a geometrical rigor, which operates automatically to penalize the abuse of force, was the main subject of Greek thought. It is the soul of the epic. Under the name of Nemesis, it functions as the mainspring of Aeschylus' tragedies. To the Pythagoreans, to Socrates and Plato, it was the jumping off point of speculation upon the nature of man and the universe. Wherever Hellenism has penetrated, we find the idea of it familiar. In Oriental countries which are steeped in Buddhism, it is perhaps this Greek idea that has lived on under the name of Karma. The Occident, however, has lost it, and no longer even has a word to express it in any of its languages: conceptions of limit, measure, equilibrium, which ought to determine the conduct of life are, in the West, restricted to a servile function, the vocabulary of technics. We are only geometricians of matter; the Greeks were, first of all, geometricians in their apprenticeship to virtue.

What can we, as writers, offer a world inviting another universal catastrophe, this time on an unprecedented scale?

First, I'd like to rehearse some personal history — if only to remind us that what appears a monolithic, irresistible darkness, is itself transient, vulnerable, and bound to change.

You recall how we met, thirty years ago, in Kyiv, at a poetry conference? The US was about to invade Iraq. The Soviet Union was on the verge of dissolution: the Iron Curtain — the term feels quaint — was about to come down. I was about to start a new teaching job, about to meet my wife-to-be in Cambridge.

I remember you, not quite thirty, standing at the podium of that lecture hall, your eloquent anger as you chastised us for assuming we, the visitors, your guests, knew something about what "you" had been through. Then, as now, you spoke for the collective — a risky strategy, yet sometimes a necessary one. In truth, neither side, neither group, knew much about each other — not the natives, not the diasporans or their children.

You see how history immediately put us into contradictory positions. You in Ukraine were about to experience the exuberance of emancipation, a cultural and intellectual renaissance such as the country had perhaps never known. We — I — on the other hand, as a citizen of the empire, was watching my country march inexorably toward yet another unwinnable war, the consequences of which continue to devastate a region "we" have been playing with for centuries — as though our superior weapons, our technology, gave us the right to act as the world's cartographers, redrawing maps to suit ourselves, with little thought for those who must live with our decisions.

You and I agree on many things; but our differences are inevitable. You were born and raised in a country under siege, its language, traditions, and faith forced underground, one which lost more people to war and famine within three devastating decades than any other country on earth, a territory which had endured centuries of occupation and repression. Entire generations of intellectuals had been decimated, murdered, imprisoned, prohibited from writing, corrupted or compelled to write in support of an experiment which went wrong from the start. I, on the other hand, grew up close to the heart — or, because I live in Boston, it's fairer to say, the brain — of the empire. It's an empire, like all others, built on the bones and the blood of the "losers" in the vocabulary favored by our president. Fortunately, here, as for you in Ukraine, there are still many people who don't subscribe to the vocabulary of triumphalism.

One thing that's certainly changed is that today the world knows of Ukraine's existence. When I was growing up people didn't believe there was such a place — it was a territory in Russia, they told me. They told me I was speaking in dialect. Today, however, I wish the word would drop off the airwaves for a while. To paraphrase Wilde, the only thing worse than not being talked about at all is being talked about all the time.

But it's clear from what our impeached president has said — his attempts to blame Ukraine for hacking the US elections — that the propaganda wars are far from over. You and I have been dealing with fake news for a long time. And so the story we are living today is intimately connected to the earlier narrative.

(Let us also acknowledge that it's sheer hypocrisy for us in the U.S. to be "shocked" that Russians tried to sway our elections. Lord knows we've been doing the same world-round for the better part of the last century: consider our actions in the Middle East, Egypt, Syria, Iran, and Saudi Arabia, not to mention in Haiti, Cuba, in Central and South America. No doubt we played favorites in Ukraine. In all those countries we have ignored ethics and principles in order to secure commercially beneficial arrangements for "our" corporations.)

But where does this leave us? What are writers, mere writers, to do in the face of such vast indifference to what we, along with billions of others, value? Humanism, we're told, belongs to the past. Today technology proposes the evolution of the "transhuman." Can we help each other in the task of imagining what might come to replace the blind worship of power? That's a question I'll take up in my next letter.

"Wisdom," observed Confucius, "lies in watching with affection the way things grow." That simple utterance, with its implication of absolute respect and even delight in the well-being of others, holds a clue to where we must look. Ok, let this be a start. More soon enough.

love,
a
january, 2020

CONTRIBUTORS

About the Translators and Editors

Marco Carynnyk is a writer, editor, documentary filmmaker, and translator. He is a former Research Fellow at the Mandel Center, where he conducted research for his project "The Pogroms of June-July 1941." With language skills in English, Ukrainian, German, Russian, and Polish, Marco Carrynnyk has translated fiction, poetry, and Soviet dissident memoirs.

McKenzie Hurder is a poet, fiction writer, and recent graduate from the University of Massachusetts Boston. Her work has been published in *Aurora Anthology*, *Fleas on the Dog*, *Rose Quartz Magazine*, *The Horny Poetry Review*, and is forthcoming in *Drunk Monkeys*. She hopes to pursue a PhD in literary theory and become a professor.

Askold Melnyczuk is the author of several novels including *The House of Widows*, *Ambassador of the Dead*, and most recently, *Smedley's Secret Guide to World Literature*. He is the founder and editor of the celebrated literary journal *Agni*, which won the Magid Award from PEN, as well as the founder of Arrowsmith Press. He is a professor of creative writing at the University of Massachusetts Boston.

MICHAEL M. NAYDAN is the Woskob Family Professor of Ukrainian Studies at Pennsylvania State University, and has over 40 books of published and edited translations to his name. He also published his literary essays in Ukrainian translation, *From Gogol to Andrukhovych*, as well as a novel about the city of Lviv, *Seven Signs of the Lion*, which appeared in Ukrainian as *Sim znakiv leva*. He's received numerous prizes for his translations, including the George S.N. Luckyj Award in Ukrainian Literature Translation.

WANDA PHIPPS is a poet, journalist, dramaturge, and translator. Her poems have appeared in countless journals such as *Agni Review*, Exquisite Corpse, and Transfer. She is the author of a chapbook, *Lunch Poems*, published by BOOG Literature, and the co-editor of *Big Bridge*, an internet Arts Zine.

LISA SAPINKOPF is the recipient of prizes from the American Translator's Association, Quarterly Review of Literature, and Columbia Translation Center. She worked as a co-translator on *Clay and Star: Contemporary Bulgarian Poets*.

DOUGLAS BURNET SMITH is the author of 16 poetry books. He has been nominated for the Governor General's Award and is a recipient of The Malahat Review Long Poem Prize. He is a professor at St. Francis Xavier University.

VIRLANA TKACZ is the founding director of the Yara Arts Group, a resident company at La MaMa Experimental Theatre in New York. She is the recipient of the National Endowment for the Arts prestigious Poetry Translation Literary Fellowship for her work in translating Serhyi Zhadan. She received a National Theatre Translation Award for her work with Wanda Phipps on Lesia Ukraina's verse play *Forest Song*.

OKSANA ZABUZHKO was born in 1960 in Lutsk, Ukraine. She earned her doctorate from the department of Philosophy at the University of Kiev in 1987. After the advent of independence in the early 1990s, she taught Ukrainian Culture as a Writer-in-Residence at Penn State University, and as a Fulbright Scholar at Harvard University and the University of Pittsburgh.

It was in Pittsburgh that she wrote *Fieldwork In Ukrainian Sex*, a novel which, upon its publication in 1996, caused the biggest literary scandal in Ukraine in decades. Since then it has been translated into sixteen languages, and recognized both as the calling card of contemporary Ukrainian literature and the "bible of Ukrainian feminism."

Zabuzhko has published a dozen more books, including three collections of stories, three volumes of essays, four books of poetry, a prize-winning study on landmark Ukrainian author, playwright, and thinker Lesia Ukrainka (1871-1913), and the prize-winning novel *The Museum of Abandoned Secrets*, which has been translated into six languages.

In 2013, together with her partner, artist Rostyslav Luzhetskyy, she established Komora, a small publishing house that supports non-commercial high-quality literature.

Her forthcoming collection of short stories, *Your Ad Could Go Here*, will be available in May 2020, and her next novel, *Cassandra's Banquet*, will debut in Winter 2021. Her *Selected Poems* is the 2020 winner of the Sundara Ramaswamy Prize for a work of poetry in translation.

ARROWSMITH is named after the late William Arrowsmith, a renowned classics scholar, literary and film critic. General editor of thirty-three volumes of *The Greek Tragedy in New Translations*, he was also a brilliant translator of Eugenio Montale, Cesare Pavese, and others. Arrowsmith, who taught for years in Boston University's University Professors Program, championed not only the classics and the finest in contemporary literature, he was also passionate about the importance of recognizing the translator's role in bringing the original work to life in a new language.

*Like the arrowsmith who turns his arrows straight and true,
a wise person makes his character straight and true.*

— Buddha

Books by

ARROWSMITH
PRESS

Girls by Oksana Zabuzhko
Bula Matari/Smasher of Rocks by Tom Sleigh
This Carrying Life by Maureen McLane
Cries of Animal Dying by Lawrence Ferlinghetti
Animals in Wartime by Matiop Wal
Divided Mind by George Scialabba
The Jinn by Amira El-Zein
Bergstein edited by Askold Melnyczuk
Arrow Breaking Apart by Jason Shinder
Beyond Alchemy by Daniel Berrigan
*Conscience, Consequence: Reflections on
Father Daniel Berrigan* edited by Askold Melnyczuk
Ric's Progress by Donald Hall
Return To The Sea by Etnairis Rivera
The Kingdom of His Will by Catherine Parnell
Eight Notes from the Blue Angel by Marjana Savka
Fifty-Two by Melissa Green
Music In—And On—The Air by Lloyd Schwartz
Magpiety by Melissa Green
Reality Hunger by William Pierce
Soundings: On The Poetry of Melissa Green edited by Sumita Chakraborty
The Corny Toys by Thomas Sayers Ellis
Black Ops by Martin Edmunds
Museum of Silence by Romeo Oriogun
City of Water by Mitch Manning
Passeggiate by Judith Baumel
Persephone Blues by Oksana Lutsyshyna
The Uncollected Delmore Schwartz edited by Ben Mazer
The Light Outside by George Kovach
The Blood of San Gennaro by Scott Harney edited by Megan Marshall
No Sign by Peter Balakian
Firebird by Kythe Heller

www.ingramcontent.com/pod-product-compliance
Lightning Source LLC
Chambersburg PA
CBHW060405080526
44583CB00012B/471